LEST WE FORGET!

Jenny

The Spirit of the Horse

Two centuries ago, when the greatest expanse of our native soil had not yet been broken by the restless feet of Euro-American settlers, more than two million proud mustangs roamed our western hills and valleys in perfect freedom. With his outstanding photographs, Robert Dawson creates idyllic images of these splendid animals as we can imagine they once were, in a frontier era that passed not so long ago. Coupled with the photos are verses, stories, essays and quips written by ardent admirers of the American horse. These writings represent three centuries of observation of our beloved crossbreed — extolling his virtues, sometimes cursing his vices, but always acknowledging his princely estate within our shores. This book honors the glory, the beauty and the spirit of the horse in America.

Photographs and Written Reflections of the American Horse
Photography by Robert Dawson - Editing by Tammy LeRoy
with a Foreword by Tanya Tucker

This book is dedicated to my parents.

Publishied by RD Publishing Inc
PO Box 44121
Phoenix, AZ 85064
(480) 483-5336
Website: dawsonphotography.com
Email: mail@dawsonphotography.com

All rights reserved ©2001. No part of this publication may be reproduced or transimitted in any form without persmission in writing from the publisher.

Photography - Robert Dawson
Text & Editing - Tammy Leroy

Design, Production, Print- Mark Kashino
KEI - Kashino Enterprises Inc
Website: kashino.com
Email: mark@kashino.com

Printed in Korea

ISBN #: 0-99678881-1-5

Acknowledgments

I would like to thank, on Robert Dawson's behalf, those whose help was indispensable in collecting photos for this book: Charlie Motley, Tanya Tucker, Billy A. Stewart, Donna Eddings, Joanna Lee, Eva Learn, Jerry and Shara Zollinger, Wade and Linda Zollinger, Sombrero Ranch, Triangle X Ranch, Lone Tree Ranch, Scenic View Ranch, Harley Bara, Andrea Waitt, Anna Lach, Laurie Barton, Erin Crane, Mike Drake, Tony Jardine, and Toby Lapp. We extend our thanks, as well, to the writers who shared with us their knowledge and their love of horses in stories and poems.

I owe a debt of gratitude also, to friends and family without whose support and forbearance I could not complete any project; and a special thanks to Allen Hazen, who taught me to love books.

Tammy LeRoy
Editor

Also published by RD Publishing: "Along the Cowboy Trail"

FOREWORD

On my fifth birthday, my father gave me my first pony. That was the beginning of my lifelong love of horses. Sometimes it feels as if I was born on horseback. Being with horses was always the most natural thing in the world to me. I'll never forget riding in the annual rodeo parade in Wilcox, Arizona from the time I was old enough to get on a horse, or the feeling I had riding through the Utah hills with my friends as a girl. Though we were not well off when I was growing up, and horses were an extravagance, we always had them.

I remember every horse I've ever had, and I've owned quite a few. Each one has its own personality and, like people, its own strengths and weaknesses. Getting along with horses is a lot like getting along with people. You have to earn their respect – you don't get it automatically. Once you have earned it, it's very rewarding. When a horse is willing to follow your instructions and even let you teach him something new, you know there is trust between you. It's an indescribable feeling when you get there, but you have to continually earn that trust. Like people, even the best horse has a bad day every now and then.

I can't imagine life without horses. There is magic about them. They have beauty, grace and amazing spirit. Robert Dawson captures that beauty and independent spirit in his photographs of horses taken in some of the most scenic places in America. From Tennessee to Wisconsin, from Montana to Arizona, he catches them being watchful, motherly, playful or calm in their most natural settings. Along with the photos, there are the heartfelt thoughts, poems and stories of people who have truly loved and understood horses. Overall, *The Spirit of the Horse* is a fitting tribute to the most magnificent animal God placed on Earth. I know you will enjoy this book.

— *Tanya Tucker*

INTRODUCTION

Two centuries ago, when the greatest expanse of our native soil had not yet been broken by the restless feet of Euro-American settlers, more than two million proud mustangs roamed our western hills and valleys in perfect freedom. These horses — the descendents of the hardy steed of the Spanish conquistador — had adapted well to the New World. They reigned over the prairies along with great, teeming herds of buffalo. Later, both Indian and white man developed breeds suitable for the work and the physical conditions of various regions of the continent, giving America's equine progeny their own special attributes. Today, more than 45,000 wild horses still roam the West, most on free range lands, under the protection of the Bureau of Land Management.

The noble horse, arguably the most beautiful of all God's creatures, has become a symbol in America of gallantry, freedom and passionate spirit. With his outstanding photographs Robert Dawson creates idyllic images of these splendid animals as we can imagine they once were, in a frontier era that passed not so long ago. The enchanting vision of horses as they appear in the wild is portrayed in Dawson's photographs, which are set in scenic locations across America, in Tennessee, Wisconsin, Illinois, Idaho, Montana, Wyoming and Arizona. As in his previous photographic work in the book, *Along the Cowboy Trail*, (R D Publishing, Inc., 2000), his eye for spectacular vistas and prime lighting make this collection of photographs of the American horse exceptional.

Coupled with the photos are verses, stories, essays and quips written by ardent admirers of the American horse. These writings represent three centuries of observation of our beloved crossbreed — extolling his virtues, sometimes cursing his vices, but always acknowledging his princely estate within our shores.

~ 4

There are much appreciated contributions to this book from contemporary writers and horse experts, including a foreword by Tanya Tucker, who is not only a legendary country music star, but also an accomplished horsewoman. There are compositions from Phil Spangeberger, a top writer for "Guns and Ammo" magazine who has also been featured in such television documentaries as A&E's "The Real West" and the History Channel's "Tales of the Gun"; from Charles Motley, a gifted horse trainer who has worked with horses on several movie sets and on the television series, "The Young Riders"; and from Jessie Mullens, Jr., editor of "American Cowboy" magazine. There is a list of the world's horses best remembered throughout history from Terri Wear, author of *The Horse's Name Was . . .*,

(Terri A. Wear, 1993). And there are inspired poems and heart-warming stories written by Jo Baeza, an award-winning journalist and author of *The Ranch Wife*, (Doubleday, 1964, University of Arizona Press, 1994), and by Christina Fleming, a veteran trainer, riding instructor, horse show judge and lecturer.

Also included in the text are cherished passages and quotes from Western documentarian Frederic Remington, Roy Rogers, Ronald Reagan and others.

Only a century ago, tens of thousands of our equine partners roamed the American landscape in swift herds, bold and unrestrained. They have been man's indispensable aides in the building of almost all civilizations, but were perhaps nowhere more essential than on this continent's vast and rugged frontier. This book honors the glory, the beauty and the spirit of the horse in America. ~

The Horse in the West

It has been said that the highways of history are paved with the bones of a horse. Certainly, the same could be said of the rugged trails that opened the American West. From the earliest days of the shaping of the frontier this noble beast played a pivotal part in transporting people and goods, in waging war, in conducting exploration and in agricultural production. Though primarily a beast of burden, the westerner's equine partner was more than just a living tool. From the beginning it served masters of every social and economic class without hesitation. The role of the horse was essential in the settling of the American West.

From the first European expeditions into the New World, the horse was a significant cog in the wheel of conquest. When Spanish conquistadors arrived in the Americas in the early 16th century, the horse, along with its worthy equine cousins; the mule, the donkey and the burro, allowed for greater exploration of the vast, untamed landscapes of Mexico and the American Southwest.

Horses and other domestic livestock were brought to the Caribbean Islands following Columbus' first voyage to the western hemisphere in 1492. The animals thrived in the lush tropical islands. The descendants of these Spanish-blooded horses, foaled in the new Spanish holdings in Santo Domingo, Cuba, Puerto Rico, and Jamaica, were used to mount military expeditions deeper into the New World. The possession of horses aided the Spanish, not only in exploration, but in gaining dominance over the aboriginal peoples they encountered.

Continued on page 14

The native peoples met by Spaniards in these new lands had never seen horses. Initially, these iron-clad men, mounted atop towering, strange and fearsome creatures, seemed godlike to the Indians, giving the conquistadors an added psychological advantage. The Old World conquerors quickly recognized the tactical benefit horses held, both in the minds of their foes and the physical advantage possessed by a mounted man in battle. Spanish law in the new territories forbid Indians to ride horses. Throughout much of the era of Spanish domination in the New World, the horse served as a symbol of Spanish authority.

The word of Spanish law however, even under the penalty of death, was not sufficient enough to keep the Native Americans afoot. In regions outside the reaches of New Spain's soldiers, Indians captured the wild descendants of horses that had escaped from the herds of earlier Spanish expeditions and colonies. With the Native Americans' eventual mastery of the horse came a new era in Indian culture in the West. Following the migration of the vast buffalo herds, the horse now gave the red man a powerful, fleet-footed animal with which he could hunt more efficiently than on foot. Horses also changed the tactics of war as it was waged by various Indian tribes. They allowed, as well, for farther travel in intertribal trade and eventually became an indispensable and much revered animal in Indian culture.

Eventually, the citizens of New Spain found a growing need for experienced horsemen to tend the swelling herds of domestic horses and cattle that thrived in the West, particularly along the Pacific coast. By the 1770s, the *Californios* found a vast labor pool of people with mixed Indian and Spanish ancestry. From this group came the vaquero, and the first true American cowboy was born. The rich ranching culture that thrived along the West Coast in the late 18th and early 19th centuries enjoyed a pastoral equine lifestyle.

Continued on page 16

With the dawning of the 19th century, the fledgling government of the United States began looking westward in the spirit of Manifest Destiny, hoping to bring under its spreading wings all lands and peoples from coast to shining coast. For the next century, the relentless push to conquer the American frontier crisscrossed the West at a full gallop. Legions of explorers arrived from the eastern states, seeking new passages westward. Pathfinders, fur trappers, army scouts and surveyors horse-backed through the untamed lands west of the Mississippi River. With the discovery of gold in California in 1848, thousands of fortune-seeking adventurers flocked to the gold fields of the Spanish West. The Yankee invaders brought with them, for better or for worse, their own civilization, altering the Californios' gracious, equestrian lifestyle forever.

Over the next several decades, other mineral discoveries created overnight "boomtowns," bringing even more emigrants to every corner of the Far West. Supplying food and other necessities to these remote centers was of immediate concern. To answer the call for beef — one of the most important staples — industrious Texans mounted fiery little mustangs and trailed longhorn cattle hundreds of miles, supplying a hungry population with meat.

Horses were also needed on the western frontier for communication and travel. For a short while, before the advent of the telegraph and the rail lines of the "iron horse," communications between East and West were maintained via the Pony Express. A series of mail routes were set up, linking the industrious East to the unsettled West with unprecedented speed. Stagecoach lines followed

Continued on page 18

old Spanish trails, bringing people and goods to the farthest reaches of the frontier.

The Native Americans – now expert and agile horsemen — were fighting the swelling masses of immigrants in a futile effort to hold on to their homelands and their ancestral ways of life. Dramatic struggles between Indians and Anglo-Americans exploded on the frontier in the mid-19th century, increasing the need for U.S. military involvement to protect the growing white population in the West. Once again, the horse took to the field as a battle tool for both red man and white. The U.S. Cavalry, with its mobility and capacity to travel greater distances than that of the footslogging infantry, provided the best means to combat the mounted warriors. For decades, both saddle-laden and bareback combatants rode their horses to the ground in a death duel for domination and survival. Eventually, all surviving Indian groups were subjugated on reservations.

Almost as quickly as it began, the West was settled. By the dawn of the 20th century, the violent "law of the gun" was replaced with the law of the courtroom. The vast herds of once numerous and free-ranging buffalo, pronghorn, elk and longhorn cattle had been supplanted by gentle herds of imported livestock. What was once considered wild country was now mostly fenced or plowed under, and its heroic native people were eeking out livings on government reservations.

Despite these changes, the horse was still present as a mode of mobility and of harnessed power. Decades later, the hard-working beast of burden would be set out to

pasture in favor of the greater "horsepower" of the gasoline engine. Here, the story of the horse in the West took on a new beginning. In Wild West shows, rodeos and films, western horses once again galloped to the forefront, into legend, and into our hearts.

Without his cowhorse, the cowboy would have been just another herdsman. Without his charger, the cavalryman was but a foot soldier. So, too, the Indian, mounted on his painted and feathered war pony, became the "Lord of the Plains." In the telling of our national story, the horse has become one of the most identifiable icons of America's frontier experience, always present in the colorful saga of the wild and woolly West of yesteryear. ~

By Phil Spangenberger

Sara

Sara, sunlight palomino,
grazes in an oak-ringed clearing
on tender shoots of meadow grass.
She lifts her head, ears turning,
to a sound of breaking branch.
Her nostrils pulse at the intruder.
Bright eyes glean movement on the hillside.
Dark, slow-gaited, nearsighted,
nosing through a manzanita thicket,
the black bear hunts for berries.
Her neck muscles quiver
As the breeze turns cold.

Jo Baeza
Holbrook, Arizona

"Horse talk" is a low grunt which seems to charm a horse and make him stand perfectly still for a moment or so at a time. It sounds like "hoh-hoh," uttered deep down in one's chest. The horse will stop his rough antics and strain motionless on the rope for a few seconds; while he is doing this and looking straight at the approaching figure, the man will wave a blanket at him and hiss at him -- "Shuh! Shuh!" It takes about fifteen minutes of this to make the horse realize that the man is harmless; that no motion which he makes, no sound that he utters, will harm him in any way.

Chief Buffalo Child Long Lance
Cardston, Alberta, Canada 1928

If ever there was a horse paradise, it was this staked plain of Texas, and here the mustangs were in all their glory -- tens of thousands of them. I have heard the number put as high as fifty thousand, and I believe that was a low estimate. These horses were well grown, larger than the mustangs in south Texas, fourteen to fifteen hands high. Some of the stallions were over fifteen hands and weighed 1,000 to 1,100 pounds.

Frank Collinson

El Paso, Texas

Originally published in Ranch Romances, March, 1936

It sure helps if you know you've got a good horse. The first time I met Trigger, I wanted to know how good a horse he was, so I got on him and turned him. Well, he could spin on a dime and give you nine cents back in change. We just fell in love. From then on, I never let him out of my sight. Finding a horse like Trigger is like finding a wife. The horse is your other half in this -- he's your partner, and he can get you out of plenty of scrapes and close calls.

Roy Rogers

I Dream Horses

I have dreamed horses for as long as I can remember. Several years ago, I dreamed of the turquoise stallion. It was daybreak and I was in a mountain cabin. I walked to the door and looked out. Drinking from a pond in the middle of a cienega was a turquoise-colored stallion with a little band of mares. He looked up at me and nickered very quietly. That was all. Years later, I was living on an old homestead on the Mogollon Rim in Arizona and found myself looking out at the same scene I had dreamed about.

Someone had given us an Arabian stallion called "Zair." He was a small desert Arabian the color cowboys call "blue." I also had a scrawny palomino filly. I liked her spirit, her gait and her looks. I called her Sara, and she was the only horse I ever loved.

Sara's bloodlines were All-American – Thoroughbred, Quarter Horse and Arabian. She grew into a headstrong beauty. She bucked for the joy of it, and she could twist like a hooked trout. She wasn't mean, but she got a big kick out of seeing how far she could throw somebody into the air. Under my husband's patient tutelage she became a good saddle horse, but she would test you, and you had better be paying attention.

When Sara was little, Zair protected her. When she came of age, he romanced her. They were inseparable. Then, one still summer night under a full moon, we heard the rage of stallions fighting and the squeals and hoofbeats of mares running up and down along the forest boundary fence. At daylight, we found the barbed wire fence laid down for half a mile, pummeled by hooves, bloodied by combat.

The black stallion was a legend in the Rim country, and he ran with his mares along the Mogollon. He had come to steal Sara, and Zair, gentle colt, had met the challenge. We found him, bruised and bloody, limping around in a corner of the meadow with Sara at his side.

Continued on page 31

He recovered quickly, but later that summer, some elk tore down the new fence we had built. Zair escaped into the National Forest. We tracked him for three days without success, but we put Sara in the corral and left the outside gate open. On the fourth morning, Zair was back in his meadow grazing contentedly with Sara and two young mares he had stolen from the black stallion. We went through the necessary paperwork and adopted them.

The wild stallion Zair had robbed was pure black with a white spot on his forehead. The Forest Service range staff had tried half-heartedly to trap the feral band for years. They competed with cattle and wildlife for forage. One year, the Forest Service trapped the magnificent stallion and his band in a strong pole corral. They were auctioned off and bound for the slaughterhouse. The buyer loaded the mares into his stock trailer, but the black charged him, teeth bared. He sent the man running and sailed over the pole corral into the forest.

In less than a year, the stallion had gathered another band of feral mares from the Fort Apache Reservation. They were swift, well-built mares with hooves like iron and well-shaped heads. Every bloodline of the horse world seemed to converge on those mustangs.

Continued on page 32

Among their ancestors were Cavalry mounts, Morgans and Steeldust horses out of Texas and Thoroughbreds raised by pioneer ranchers. This was all added to a base of Spanish mustang originating from 400 years of Apache raids on Mexico. There was no sight more enchanting than that of the black stallion nipping at his mares, keeping them in line as they raced through the forest. He was the stallion I had dreamed of, I was sure.

Sadly, the following year, the black stallion and five of his mares were gunshot by someone and left to die an agonizing death in a meadow where they had been grazing. The same summer, our captured bay mare foaled. She had a pure black colt with a white spot on his forehead. We named him "Sabache," an Indian word for obsidian. The blood of the black stallion still runs strong in horses all over Arizona and New Mexico.

In the years to come, Sara and I formed an unbreakable bond. She carried me over some rough country in the White Mountains and on the Blue River, without ever flinching. If a cliff was steep, she would slide down on her rump. If a river was flooded, she would find a place to cross. I could give her her head and she would take me home through the blackest night.

She was also a devoted mother. Sometimes I would take Sara, her baby and her two-year-old filly out for a picnic. The dogs would baby-sit the little ones while I washed Sara off in the creek and let her roll in the grass. Those days were as close to perfect as it gets.

My next dream was a nightmare. I was keeping Sara, now 22, on a pasture in New Mexico while her filly was being trained. I dreamed she was running back and forth, calling to me. The next day I called the people who were taking care of her, and they said they would check on her. A day later, they called back to say they found her lying in the pasture. Sara was dead.

I did not want any horses after that. I lived in town and thought horses belonged on a ranch where they could run free. Then Molly showed up. I woke up one morning to find a half-starved bay mare with a broken nose looking in my kitchen window. She had a brand almost as big as she

Continued on page 35

was and scar tissue on one foot, but she was young and sound. I caught her and took her back to my neighbor's place. He said he had bought her because he felt sorry for her. He was going to get her back into shape and sell her. The next morning she was back on my porch.

I paid him $300 and put her in the big lot next to my house. The first time I saddled her, she shied a little, but I led her down to the forest gate at the end of my street and climbed aboard. It took about five seconds for me to realize she had never been ridden. I got off and thought about it, then got back on. We worked it out together. In the spring, she dropped a perfect foal I named Rosa.

Eventually, a sad day came when I sold the two horses to my best friend because I could no longer ride. But I have seen the wild horses run, and I have ridden in the wind and sun. I am content to dream horses, now. And I know Sara is waiting for me somewhere. ~

by Jo Baeza

The Bronco

He graces the Western landscape not because he reminds us of the equine ideal but because he comes of the soil and has borne the heat and the burden and the vicissitudes of all that pale of romance which will cling about the Western frontier. . . . He has borne the Moor, the Spanish conqueror, the red Indian, the mountain man, and the *vaquero* through all the glories of their careers; but they will soon be gone, with all their heritage of gallant deeds. The pony must meekly enter the new regime. He must wear the collar of the new civilization and earn his oats by the sweat of his flank. There are no more worlds for him to conquer; now he must till the ground.

Frederic Remington
"Horses of the Plain," in Century Magazine
January, 1889

If you want to find horses, go to the prettiest place in reach, and there you'll almost always find them. Horses love beauty as much as humans do.

Eugene Manlove Rhodes
Bar Cross Ranch, New Mexico
1930

Ghosts in the Sagebrush

It has been said that on the far range land,

live the wild ones who wear no brand.

Ghosts in the sagebrush, creeping from the twilight,

driven from the secret pastures to wander the trails of their kind,

with only one mission in mind —

To be wild,

to be wild ,

to be wild.

Their only thought,

to live on the edge and never be caught.

Charles Motley

Phoenix, Arizona

Miracle on Horseback

When "Catherine" was brought to me for therapeutic riding lessons, she was functioning at the level of a ten-month-old child. Once a beautiful, bright and active little girl, a tragic automobile accident left her with serious brain injuries. She was left unable to stand, to feed herself, or to communicate. She did not acknowledge the presence of those close to her.

Catherine's mother never lost hope. She enrolled her daughter, who was then 15, in the therapeutic riding class where I was a student teacher. I had been a riding instructor for years and I thought it would be the easiest part of the certification course — until I saw Catherine's mother push the girl's wheelchair into the barn. Catherine was held upright in the chair by nylon straps, helplessly dependent on others for every need. Looking at the beautiful child with her listless limbs and dark, blank eyes was heart wrenching. Her mother explained how the head injury had affected Catherine. Her body, though uninjured, received no information from the brain. Catherine stared lifelessly, seemingly unaware of anything around her.

Some volunteers and I placed Catherine's chair on the mounting ramp next to an aged gelding named Ticker — a veteran therapy horse. He was especially patient with riders who had to be lifted from wheel chairs onto his strong, broad back. Once an accomplished Western show horse, a generous family had donated Ticker to the therapy program. He seemed to know the importance of his job from the first day he arrived. Horses seem inexplicably sensitive to the needs of people with disabilities.

Continued on page 53

Three of us lowered Catherine onto the English saddle. We slid her new riding boots into the stirrups, placed the reins in her tightly clenched hands and did our best to help her sit up without a chair or straps to support her.

Catherine's prospects of being able to ride a horse didn't look good. Still, I decided to try letting Ticker take a few steps, knowing it would take constant support from the horse and the volunteers to keep her from falling off. One person led Ticker, two supported Catherine's back, and I talked to her as if it were just another lesson with any other teenage girl.

Then, something remarkable occurred. With each new step of the horse, we watched Catherine sit taller and taller in the saddle. Her body no longer jerked back and forth from the motion of the horse, but was rhythmically moving to the lovely, four-beat walk of a well-bred horse. Within minutes, Catherine was riding without any assistance. She held her head appropriately and gazed ahead to the next section of the arena. She seemed aware of my instructions and rode better with every step. I continued to give directions as if I had expected her to do well, yet along with the others, I was in disbelief. Our only disappointment was that she was refused to hold one rein in each hand, which is proper form in English riding style. She repeatedly tossed away the rein in her right hand and then placed that arm quietly at her side, despite the volunteer's persistence in placing the rein back into Catherine's hand.

Continued on page 55

I glanced toward the stands and saw her mother's joyful tears. She was as amazed as the rest of us at her daughter's accomplishment. Then I looked at Catherine and saw tears streaming down the child's face too.

I spoke with her mother following the lesson and learned that Catherine had shown horses in a 4-H club prior to the accident. She had loved Western events and had refused to show in English classes. I saw many such "miracles" in the years that followed while I worked with the disabled as a therapeutic riding instructor, but the memory of Catherine and the horse that was able to help break through her lonely, isolated world will always stay with me. ~

Christina Fleming

The golden age of the bronco was ended some twenty years ago [in the 1860s] when the great tidal wave of Saxonism reached his grassy plains. He was rounded up and brought under the yoke by the thousand, and his glories departed. Here and there a small band fled before man, but their freedom was hopeless. The act of subjugation was more implied than real, and to this day as the cowboy goes out and drives up a herd of broncos to the corral, there is little difference between the wild horse of old and his enslaved progeny. . . .

Frederic Remington
"Horses of the Plain," in Century Magazine
January, 1889

The Horse's Name Was . . .

ALGONQUIN — A calico Icelandic pony owned by Archibald Roosevelt, son of President Theodore Roosevelt. Once when Archibald was sick, the pony was taken upstairs in the White House to his bedroom.

APACHE — One of the horses Kit Carson rode while he was Fremont's messenger from California to Washington, D.C., in the 1840s.

BABIECA — The white war-horse belonging to the Spanish warrior-knight Rodrigo in the 11th century. Rodrigo was nicknamed el Sidi or El Cid Campeador. BABIECA, also spelled BAVIECA, means "idiot." El Cid named him that when people called him an idiot for choosing the scraggly colt. BABIECA was made to carry his dead master's body strapped upright in the saddle from a besieged city, which made the enemy think that El Cid had risen from the dead. BABIECA lived to be 40 years old and died 2 1/2 years after his master.

BLACK BEAUTY — The black horse in Anna Sewell's 1877 book, *Black Beauty*. The book was written to protest cruel treatment of carriage horses.

Continued on page 61

BLACK JACK — The big black Thoroughbred with a star on its forehead was a ceremonial horse for the United States Army. He was never ridden, but was led riderless in many funeral processions, including those of Herbert Hoover, John F. Kennedy, Douglas MacArthur and Lyndon B. Johnson. BLACK JACK died at the age of 29.

BLIND TOM — A blind gelding that pulled flatcars for the Union Pacific Railroad around 1866.

Continued on page 63

BUCEPHALUS — The favorite mount of Alexander the Great, it was a black stallion with a white triangle on his forehead that resembled an ox head. BUCEPHALUS means "ox head." Young Alexander tamed the horse and rode him in all his conquests. He founded the city of Bucephala around 326 B.C., named in honor of the horse after it died of a war injury at the site. The horse was buried in an alabaster tomb. Alexander the Great died two years later.

BUCKSHOT – James Butler "Wild Bill" Hickok's horse in real life and in the television show "Wild Bill Hickok," 1952-1958. Hickok was a U.S. Marshal.

BUCKSKIN JOE — A large yellow horse that William F. "Buffalo Bill" Cody rode during his early scouting and hunting trips. Cody won the Congressional Medal of Honor after an Indian fight in which he rode BUCKSKIN JOE. The horse was retired after he went blind following a 195-mile ride in which Cody escaped from pursuing Indians. BUCKSKIN JOE died in 1882 of old age.

Continued on page 64

BURNS – Union General George B. McClellan's tall black horse during the Civil War. The horse would wheel in the midst of battle to head back to the stable when it was time for dinner. The general developed the McClellan military saddle.

BUTTERMILK – The buckskin gelding owned by Dale Evans, which she rode on television on "The Roy Rogers Show," from 1951 - 1964.

CHAMPION — Gene Autry's palomino horse that starred in western movies and in the 1950 television show, "The Adventures of Champion." CHAMPION was called the "World's Wonder Horse" and his hoofprints can be found in front of Grauman's Chinese Theater in Hollywood.

CINCINNATI — The 17-hand, dark bay Saddle Horse-type charger that carried Union General Ulysses S. Grant during the Civil War. Also spelled CINCINNATUS. He was a gift to Grant from a dying man in Cincinnati, Ohio. CINCINNATI was sired by LEXINGTON, a Thoroughbred racer. Grant once refused $10,000 in gold for him. President Lincoln once rode him. After the war, CINCINNATI retired to a farm and died in 1878.

Continued on page 66

EBENEZER – Chief Joseph's war-horse in the late 1800's. It was a light roan Appaloosa with red spots and it was a good racehorse.

EBONY – President Abraham Lincoln rode this black stallion during a review of the troops in 1864. Some artillery fire startled EBONY, who bolted. The stallion was eventually stopped by an orderly, and Lincoln was able to finish the review. EBONY had been loaned to him for the occasion by General Benjamin Butler.

FIRPON – The tallest horse on record, a Percheron-Shire crossbreed owned by Julio Falabella. The horse stood 21.1 hands high and died in 1972 at the age of 13. Falabella also owned miniature horses.

FRITZ – The pinto cow horse that worked with Williams S. Hart in early western movies and lived to the age of 31. Hart and FRITZ used no stunt doubles for their 1920s movies, which included *Pinto Ben* and *The Narrow Trail*. Hart's horse CACTUS KATE and pack mule LISABETH were devoted to the gelding FRITZ.

Continued on page 08

GERONIMO – Horse ridden 2,500 miles by 6-year-old Templeton Abernathy to meet Colonel Teddy Roosevelt in 1910. The trip from Oklahoma to New York took Templeton, his 10-year-old brother Louis, and Louis's horse SAM, six weeks to complete.

GLADSTONE – The horse that drew the Cherrelyn car in Englewood, Colorado around 1904. GLADSTONE would draw the car to the top of the hill and then jump onto the platform on his own for the ride back down the hill.

JUMBO – A big bay gelding owned by Lederle Laboratories. JUMBO gave blood for tetanus antitoxin and pneumonia antiserum from 1929 to 1940. He died in 1944 and a plaque was erected in memory of his service to humanity.

LUCY LONG – A 15-hand, gentle sorrel mare ridden by Confederate General Robert E. Lee during the Civil War; a gift from General "Jeb" Stuart. Lee called her MISS LUCY. She had a fast walk and an easy canter but not enough stamina to be used constantly as a war horse. One story says she broke her picket line to mate with a stallion and had to be sent back to the farm, while another said she broke down in battle. She was lost for several years, but Lee found her later and kept her. LUCY LONG died in 1891 at age 39.

Continued on page 70

MAN O'WAR – A famous chestnut stallion foaled in 1917, owned by Samuel Riddle, and bred by August Belmont. MAN O'WAR was one of the greatest racehorses ever. His nickname was BIG RED. His pedigree could be traced back to the Godolphin Arabian. He was difficult to train and disliked being saddled. MAN O'WAR won both the Preakness and the Belmont in 1920. He never ran in the Kentucky Derby as it was not then as highly regarded as it is now. He sired other famous racehorses, such as WAR ADMIRAL. He was auctioned off as a yearling for $5,000. He lost only one race, to UPSET, in 1919, after having been mishandled at the barrier and facing the wrong direction when the race started. MAN O'WAR damaged a tendon and was retired in 1921. He was visited by many people before he died of colic at age 26 in 1947, less then one month after his devoted groom, Will Harbut, died. He was originally buried at Faraway Farms, but his remains were moved to a horse park in 1976.

NELSON – The favorite mount of George Washington; a big-boned, chestnut gelding with a white face and legs. He was a gift from the governor of Virginia, Thomas Nelson, Jr., in 1765. Washington hunted with him for ten years until the war started and then found him to be good in battle. Washington rode him at Valley Forge. NELSON was still alive in 1785 at the age of 23 when a census of Washington's stable showed he had 130 horses. No paintings were done of the horse.

THE PACING WHITE MUSTANG – A legendary wild, white stallion claimed to have been seen from the Rio Grande to the Rocky Mountains. One story said that a young girl who had been strapped to the back of an old mare behind a pioneer wagon had fallen asleep and gotten lost. According to the story, THE PACING WHITE MUSTANG helped her get back to her family.

PRINCE CHARLIE – The large-boned, bay horse ridden by Jack Jouett during the American Revolution. Jouett made a dangerous sixty-mile ride on PRINCE CHARLIE in order to warn Thomas Jefferson at Monticello that the British were coming. Also called PRINCE CHARLES.

Continued on page 72

PUTNAM – The army horse decorated by General Pershing as the best artillery horse in the American Expeditionary Forces in France during World War I.

RECKLESS – A small Korean racing mare that served as an ammunition carrier for a U.S. Marine platoon during the Korean War. It was a 4-year-old, 14-hand mare with a blaze and three white socks. The horse was trained by Lieutenant Eric Pedersen to carry 75mm shells. It made 51 solitary runs for ammunition during the battle of Vegas, carrying six to ten rounds of ammunition each trip. The horse received a medal for bravery under fire and was promoted to Marine Sergeant in 1954.

SHOTGUN – A small, sturdy, saddle pony mare ridden by Albert Smith of Port Angeles, Washington, into a raging sea to pull a lifeboat full of stranded men to shore in 1930. The horse was nominated for the Latham Foundation Gold Medal for animal heroes in 1931.

TONY – The sorrel with white stockings and blazed face that was owned and ridden by early western movie star, Tom Mix. TONY starred in many movies, including the 1922 movie, *Just Tony*, based on a story by Max Brand. TONY was often called "Tony the Wonder Horse." Mix and Tony did not use doubles in their movies. The horse's hoofprints are in the sidewalk outside Grauman's Chinese Theater in Hollywood. Tom rode a younger horse, TONY JR., after TONY was retired. Tom Mix died in a car accident in 1940, and TONY died at age 34, in 1944.

TOPPER – William "Hopalong Cassidy" Boyd's showy white horse, seen in the 1948 television show, "Hopalong Cassidy." TOPPER also starred in Cassidy's early western movies.

TRAVELLER – The favorite, iron-gray Saddlebred warhorse of Confederate General Robert E. Lee. The spirited gelding had a black mane and tail and was purchased by Lee in the mid-1800s for $200. He had been named JEFF DAVIS and GREENBRIER before Lee renamed him TRAVELLER. Lee rode him during the Civil War and was very devoted to the horse although other people said it was difficult to ride. TRAVELLER marched in Lee's funeral procession in 1870 and died within two years later from an infected nail-puncture wound. It was buried on the campus of Washington and Lee University in Virginia, but later its bones were unearthed and exhibited at the museum on the campus.

Continued on page 74

TRIGGER – The golden palomino with white mane, tail and stocking that was ridden by Roy Rogers in 87 western movies. The horse was also starred on "The Roy Rogers Show" on television for six and a half years. TRIGGER knew 50 tricks, was housebroken for tours, and often stole the show from Roy. Star of the 1946 movie *My Pal Trigger*, it was said to be the smartest horse in the movies. Its hoofprints are in front of Grauman's Chinese Theater in Hollywood. The horse lived into its early 30s and died in 1965. TRIGGER was stuffed and is now displayed at the Roy Rogers-Dale Evans Museum in Victorville, California.

TRUXTON – A racehorse purchased by Andrew Jackson to race against GREYHOUND in order to pay off Jackson's debts. TRUXTON won, and Jackson went on to become president.

UNKNOWN HORSE – The name of the horse Paul Revere rode on his historic midnight ride, April 18, 1775, has never been known for sure, although some say its name was BROWN BEAUTY. It is known only that it was a light and sure-footed, chestnut, Narragansett pacer mare of good quality, borrowed from Deacon John Larkin's stable.. Revere warned John Adams and John Hancock in Lexington that the British were coming. Revere and the mare were later captured by the British, who kept the mare. ~

Terri Wear
"The Horses Name Was..."
(Terry A. Wear, 1993)

Nothing scares a horse quicker than a quiet thing that moves toward him and makes no noise. He will jump and break his neck at a noisy movement of a rodent in the grass or a falling twig, while a roaring buffalo or a streaming train will pass him unnoticed. That is because he has the same kind of courage that man has: Real courage, the courage to face any odd that he can see and hear and cope with, but a superstitious fear of anything ghostlike.

Chief Buffalo Child Long Lance
Cardston, Alberta, Canada 1928

Is it the wind those branches stirs?
No, no! from out the forest prance
    A trampling troop; I see them come!
In one vast squadron they advance!
    I strove to cry, — my lips were dumb.
The steeds rush on in plunging pride;
But where are they the reins to guide?
A thousand horse, — and none to ride!
With flowing tail, and flying mane,
Wide nostrils, never stretched by pain,
Mouths bloodless to the bit or rein,
And feet that iron never shod,
And flanks unscarred by spur or rod,
A thousand horse, the wild, the free,
Like waves that follow o'er the sea,
    Came thickly thundering on, . . .

Headed by one black mighty steed,
Who seemed the patriarch of his breed,
    Without a single speck or hair
Of white upon his shaggy hide;
They snort, they foam, neigh, swerve aside,
And backward to the forest fly,
By instinct, from a human eye.

Lord Byron
From Mazeppa's Ride

In his intelligence the bronco has no equal, unless it is the mule. That hybrid has an extra endowment of brains, as though in compensation for the beauty which he lacks. . . . It would be quite unfair to his fellows to institute anything like a comparison without putting in evidence the peculiar method of defense to which he resorts when he struggles with man for the mastery. Everyone knows that he bucks, and familiarity with that characteristic never breeds contempt. . . .

Frederic Remington
"Horses of the Plain," in Century Magazine
January, 1889

Dream Horses

In the deep cave of night

before dawn,

I dream horses.

A sleek remuda mills in a meadow

beneath a bristling ridge.

A gathering of spirits

from the corners of the wind.

I see the horses of my youth

and call to each of them —

bays, sorrels, buckskins, greys.

Across a silent stream

welling from a mossy seep

I see my chestnut gelding

with flaxen mane and tail.

I cross the stream

and touch his nose with mine

smell his clover breath,

hear his trembling sigh,

then notice he is standing saddled.

As joy throbs in my throat,

I swing into the saddle.

Small and lithe, a mustang out of Mexico,

the wariest steer could not

escape the fleetness of his hooves.

I turn him toward the rimrocks

high above the somber forest

Where we can smell the rain

And ride the clouds.

Jo Baeza
Holbrook, Arizona

The White Steed of the Prairies

. . . Every range had its own superb mustang, but supreme above the local superiors was the White Mustang of the Prairies. All men who rode horses in the mustang world knew of him, talked of him, wanted him

This ubiquitous stallion went under many names: The Pacing White Stallion, the White Steed of the Prairies, the White Mustang, the White Sultan, the Ghost Horse of the Plains, the Phantom Wild Horse. Whatever his name, he answered to none. His fire, his grace, his beauty, his speed, his endurance, his intelligence were the attributes that men commonly admire most in horses, but in him they were supernal; his passion for liberty was the passion that his admirers and pursuers idealized most constantly, both in the abstract and in themselves.

From Tales of the Mustang, *by J. Frank Dobie. Copyright, 1936, by J. Frank Dobie. Dallas: The Book Club of Texas.*

Unless he be tied up to a post, no one ever knew an Indian pony to die of the cold. With his front feet he will paw away the snow to an astonishing depth in order to get at the dry herbage, and by hook or by crook he will manage to come through the winter despite the wildest prophecies on the part of the uninitiated that he cannot live ten days in such a storm.

Frederic Remington
"Horses of the Plain," in Century Magazine
January, 1889

The wild horse can see, hear, and smell a man farther than any other animal, except a woman.

Frank M. Lockard
Norton, Kansas
From "Black Kettle," published by R.G. Wolfe, 1924

I've often said there's nothing better for the inside of a man than the outside of a horse.

— Ronald Reagan

"America has been generously blessed with nature's gifts. Horses and children are among the best of these."
— Tom Tumas